# Chapter 1

# INTRODUCTION

Your on-the-job survival depends on more than just getting the job done in a competent manner. It also requires your demonstration of effective employee relations skills. Regardless of your proven technical abilities, you stand a chance of losing your job if you cannot:

- adjust to imperfections in the job

- deal constructively with work-related problems

- establish a sound and secure working relationship with your boss

- receive and accept managerial criticism in a non-defensive manner

- resolve, or at least effectively manage, conflicts with co-workers

- win support of influential people within your organization

- establish personal and professional credibility, acquire the image of a person who possesses practical knowledge, reflects high character and demonstrates good will toward others

If you want to survive and thrive on the job, you must display self-management skills. Self-management requires withstanding or tolerating the common frustrations that are part of your job. It means accepting the limitations of your boss and fellow employees and working within them. It is learning how to get understanding and cooperation from others so that your job is made more satisfying. When you practice self-management, you pay attention to what is right and good within your organization as well as what is wrong. You realize that your number one objective on the job is to be successful, not necessarily happy. Happiness on the job is usually a by-product of success.

As Vice President, Human Resource Services at Weiss Memorial Hospital, Chicago, Illinois, I counsel employees on all levels to help them gain a greater measure of job effectiveness and satisfaction. I have observed many employees who have manipulated and distorted reality to conform to some fantasy about how the job *should* be. I have heard their unrealistic expectations of what their boss or co-workers *should* do for them. I have seen how employees set themselves up for frustration and failure.

At every opportunity, I share with employees how to steer clear of self-defeating behaviors and how to get off the collision course on which they are headed. I try to instill in employees a sense of responsibility for the impact that they have on others. I view them as adults who must be accountable for their actions. I never buy into an employee's perception that he is captive or victim to a problem situation, regardless of how eloquently he feigns helplessness.

If you are like most employees with whom I interact, you are hungry for on-the-job survival strategies. Everthing in the media today seems to focus on how to get a job, not how to keep one. This book provides practical and immediately useful advice on employee relations issues to maximize you chances for ON·THE·JOB·SURVIVAL.

# Chapter 2

# DEALING EFFECTIVELY WITH YOUR WORK PROBLEMS

On the job problems usually stem from your expectations unfulfilled by co-workers, boss, the nature of the work, or conditions on the job. Something is simply not happening the way you think it should, could, or must. The difference between *what is happening* and *what you expected to happen* causes concern, discomfort or insecurity on the job.

Your initial response to a work-related problem may not necessarily be the best way to resolve it. Before you take any significant steps you may regret, consider answering the following questions:

**1. Am I into an immediate gratification kick?** Solving a problem often requires patience. You can usually influence a co-worker and shape events in a positive direction if you go about it in the right way and allow enough time. This requires a willingness to "chip away" at a problem and give the change process a chance to unfold naturally. Even if the problem cannot be resolved immediately, a few meaningful gestures that communicate a willingness to meet your co-workers halfway can reap significant results.

**2. Am I expecting perfection in my co-workers or boss?**
If you have "out of this world" expectations of other people, you
will never be satisfied. Your failure will stem from your inability
to accept the fact that co-workers and the boss are human, each
with unique set of strengths and limitations.

**3. Am I so busy finding fault and openly criticizing
someone else that I have no time left to look at my own
need to change?** It's a strange thing, but those employees who
are very judgmental toward peers or their boss are usually
masters at making excuses for their own mistakes and limitations.

**4. Have I anticipated and planned for resistance to my
ideas?** No matter how well you explain yourself, some
employees are likely to misunderstand or misinterpret your
statements. This is understandable. There exists a wide variety
of normal and legitimate reasons for co-workers to question your
arguments. But you will have a better chance of persuading
colleagues to consider your viewpoint if you think through all of
their possible objections *before* you approach them. Predict the
questions they might ask and have available answers. Be
prepared to:

- Explain yourself calmly and rationally.

- Be honest and direct, but respect co-workers' feelings,
  particularly if they may disagree with you.

- Discuss alternative ways of solving your problem or
  achieving your goal.

- Establish a climate of non-competitiveness and trust.
  This can only be achieved if you are perceived to be
  dealing with co-workers "in good faith;" you maintain
  confidentiality, you are sensitive to their work needs,
  you do not deliberately distort their messages or question
  their integrity.

**5. Am I practicing empathy?** Empathy is the ability to accurately predict what a co-worker will say or do as a result of how you approach him. If you are constantly surprised or dismayed by the responses you evoke in someone, then you are probably having trouble empathizing. Without realizing it, your bold assertions or accusations may be interpreted by your colleague as aggression and hostility. Or you may be giving off frequent "now hear this" messages that are interpreted as grandstanding and ego-tripping.

The empathy approach calls for "planned uncertainty" regarding what is the best action to take for solving the problem. When you empathize, you present your ideas as perceptions rather than absolute truths. You *welcome* a co-worker's differing ideas and consider them seriously. You demonstrate a willingness to accommodate someone and to change when necessary to achieve cooperation. Your desire to establish an effective working relationship is greater than your need to embarrass, inconvenience, harm, or dominate a co-worker.

Of course, even if you do empathize, you will inevitably engage in some discussions that result in disharmony and ill will. When this happens, try to "regroup" and determine what factors contributed to this conflict. Begin by looking at your own behavior to see if you unintentionally escalated or aggravated the problem. Try to remember what specifically you said and the *manner* in which you said these things. Recall how the co-worker responded. What ideas "turned him on" or "ticked him off." Armed with this analysis, approach the co-worker again when the time and place are advantageous for a candid and confidential discussion. But this time, consider changing your approach to increase the odds of getting what you want.

# Choosing Your Battles with Discretion

You should be careful not to "go to the mat" on every problem that you identify. If you continuously complain, you run the risk of being labeled a troublemaker or agitator. And when a really serious problem emerges that needs attention, it will not be given the consideration it requires. Therefore, choose your "battles" with discretion. Before you blow the whistle on a problem, ask yourself the following questions:

1. Is the problem really solvable? Am I hitting my head against the wall about a problem no one, including my boss, can do anything about? Am I being a Don Quixote, tilting at windmills, immersing myself in self-righteous indignation?

2. How serious is the problem? Have I done everything I can to adjust to it by minimizing its negative impact?

3. How permanent is the problem? Will it solve itself in time if I do nothing?

4. Am I upset about something that's not really my problem? Could I be butting into someone else's turf when it's actually none of my business?

5. Have I examined my share of responsibility for this problem? Even if I didn't start the problem, am I contributing to it in some way? Am I so busy blaming and shaming my co-workers or boss, for example, that I fail to see how I may be escalating the conflict? Am I feeling sorry for myself as a victim of circumstance or a captive to the situation? Am I playing the martyr? Am I simply dumping the problem in another person's lap?

**6.** Have I exhausted all problem solving efforts with those who can most directly do something about the problem? Am I willing to face the person with whom I have difficulty for honest, direct and constructive dialogue?

**7.** Is someone else in a better position to deal with the problem? If so, why am I sticking *my* neck out? Have I identified who has the influence, power, or control within my organization to assist me in addressing the issue?

**8.** Am I looking for a quick fix solution to a complex problem? Do I fully understand the magnitude and scope of the issue, or am I simply looking at how it affects me? Should I get more information so that I can speak with greater authority on the subject?

**9.** Are my continued efforts to deal with the problem eroding an important working relationship? Are my attempts at altering the situation creating more resistance? Are people digging their heels, becoming more inflexible or defensive? Is it clear that my co-workers or boss are truly ready for a change?

**10.** What is my chance of winning if I engage in a "toe-to-toe" battle with my co-workers or boss on this issue? Is the problem so critical to me that I am willing to pull all the stops to get what I want? Is this the "hill I am willing to die on" — the one I am willing to go down fighting for?

In the normal course of the day, when confronted with a problem, it is not realistic to expect someone to run down this entire list of questions. But it is always helpful and productive to review these issues before deciding on a course of action. Your co-workers and boss are more likely to view you as a responsible individual in your attempts to resolve conflict.

# Notes

# Chapter 3

# ESTABLISHING REALISTIC EXPECTATIONS OF OTHERS

*"Let me have the determination to change what I can change, the serenity to accept what I cannot and the wisdom to know the difference between the two."* [1]

In their book, *A New Guide to Rational Living*, Albert Ellis and Robert Harper followed in the tradition of St. Francis of Assisi when they suggested that you should have the courage to deal with those frustrations in life that can be minimized or eliminated. But whether you like it or not, some things are out of your control and it is better to gracefully accept reality when you cannot change it. [2]

You probably don't have the power to control your co-workers or boss regardless of how well or often you try to reason with them. Every person is looking out for his own self-interests, in search of ways to make his job easier, more satisfying and effective. If one of your co-workers chooses to act irresponsibly, that is his problem, not yours, unless you allow yourself to get "sucked" into his negative behavior. If you act in a similarly counter-productive fashion, then *you* become part of the problem.

Don't let a colleague "get your goat." Don't allow yourself to be provoked into any irresponsible behavior that will result in corrective action against you. Maintain a sense of responsibility for your behavior regardless of any irrational statements or actions made against you. Your co-worker cannot make you act hostile or ugly unless you choose to act that way. And remember, if someone has control over your emotions, he has control over you.

Don't get involved in "personality conflicts" on the job. Distinguish between liking or disliking a co-worker on a personal level and the necessity of working effectively with this person. So what if you are not the best of friends, you're a professional with a job to do and an important role to play. You are responsible for delivering a product or providing a service. Therefore your personal feelings must always take a back seat to task completion and goal accomplishment.

Try to remain flexible and composed when a co-worker or boss is placing demands upon you. Your objective is to solve a problem and maintain a workable relationship, not to win or dominate. Always try to focus upon the specific work-related issues, even if the co-worker is taking the "low road" by hitting below the belt. Don't use words that inflame. If you know a person well enough, you are aware of what statements or actions on your part will rattle or trigger him off. Be equally certain that your "non-verbal" communication (your tone of voice, volume, rate of speech, facial expression and overall body posture) does not express ridicule or sarcasm. Be mindful that your non-verbal messages can have greater impact and convey a totally different message than what you actually say.

The bottom line is this: if in response to a co-worker or manager's provoking actions, you lose control, become intent on getting even, or try to fight fire with fire, you have allowed him to get the better of you. If you become unduly aroused, upset, and negative because a colleague is acting inappropriately, you get sidetracked from your main concern: the way *you* behave, the things *you* do.[3]

## Adjusting to Imperfections

Your efforts should be aimed at maintaining realistic expectations of persons with whom you work. Any attempts to change working conditions that are truly unalterable is a terrible waste of your time and resources and a "set up" for frustration and failure. We are living in an imperfect world. There is no place on earth where utopia can be found. No work place exists that does not include some undesirable elements with which a person must learn to cope.

Most working conditions are marked by frustrations and irritations of varying degrees. Your concerns or aggravations may indeed be greater than others normally experience. Try to overcome these problems if they are truly resolvable. But if the problems are 1) inevitable, 2) an inherent condition of the work, or 3) outside your control, an all out attempt to adjust and accommodate yourself to the situation should be made.

Are your expectations of others realistic? Can you adjust to the job's imperfections? To determine the answer to these questions, follow the steps outlined below:

**Step 1:** Make a laundry list of all those things about the job and the people with whom you work that you truly appreciate. These are the factors that keep you coming back to work and contribute to your overall satisfaction on the job. Even those employees with whom you are experiencing problems possess certain positive qualities. You should acknowledge these and include them in this list.

**Step 2:** Make a laundry list of those things about the job that are unpleasant. These are the factors that limit or inhibit your job satisfaction or performance. Also, determine which of these undesirable work factors is within your control to change and which ones are unalterable.

**Step 3:** Review the above lists and objectively compare the advantages versus the disadvantages of remaining in your present job.

If the advantages of staying in your present position outweigh the immediate need to separate from it, then resolve to:

1. Overcome those frustrations that can be changed

2. Adjust to those frustrations that are unresolvable and try to minimize their negative impact

3. Learn to appreciate and take full advantage of the positive factors that do exist on the job.

Every day when you wake up, get dressed and travel to work, you have made an important decision that at least for today, the job is worth coming to. Therefore, you might as well make the best of it until you decide that this job is not for you and you are prepared to move on to something different. Until then, make an all out effort to be productive and constructive in your present job.

Most important, if you do decide to remain in your present capacity, don't view yourself as captive to your situation. As an adult, you have chosen to work where you do. Economic conditions may limit your options to do something else, but for now it does little good (and much harm) to feel sorry, resent yourself and others around you, and hit your head against the wall reminding yourself about how bad things are. Agonizing about the job's imperfections is almost always self-defeating. You won't like yourself, and you will be difficult to work with. Your general negative attitude will cause others to react in a negative way toward you. Your behavior influences their behavior, and it is very possible that your depression or hostility will prevent you from successfully dealing with those work problems that are within your control.

## Determining When It's Time to Quit

Perhaps the problems that you experience are so serious or all consuming that they cast a shadow over the positive elements of the job. Perhaps you truly cannot adjust to or tolerate the frustrations that result from coming to work. The advantages of staying simply don't outweigh the disadvantages. If this is the case, it's time to separate from your job.

Resigning from a position should be viewed as a last resort, an action to be taken only after exhausting all attempts to resolve the problem. But sometimes quitting makes the most sense, particularly if your negative attitude results in behavior that is harmful to yourself and aggravating to others.

A voluntary resignation from your job is also very practical if you find yourself on a collision course with your boss. Try to avoid at all costs the disgrace of getting fired. Don't place yourself in a position of losing control over your own career. Don't allow your boss to decide for you when to stay or leave. Separate from the job under your own terms and conditions when the time is right for you.

Until you find a better job, play it straight. Do what is expected of you and more. Prove to yourself, co-workers and the boss that you can rise above the differences of opinion, the personality disputes and daily irritations of the job. Demonstrate a willingness and ability to perform your tasks in a more than competent manner. Don't threaten your job security by acting in a way that communicates to others: "I could not care less about losing this job." In short, don't burn the bridges behind you.

Consider your present job as a link in the chain or a springboard for finding a position that is more suitable to your needs. Don't kid yourself that if you are forced out of the job under a cloud of suspicion, distrust and hostility that you will increase your chances of landing a more desirable position. Most companies do not look kindly at transferring a troublemaker from one place in the organization to another. And your boss always has the power to give a bad reference, making it difficult for you to "land on your feet" elsewhere within a reasonable time frame.

If you have determined that sooner or later you will be separating from your present job, make every effort to temporarily adjust to the problems you face. Don't spend a great deal of energy complaining about the situation making yourself and everyone around you miserable. Don't threaten your boss by delivering an ultimatum (however subtle) that you will quit unless your problems are immediately eliminated. She is likely to call your bluff and the smart money bets on things being resolved in the boss' favor.

# Chapter 4

# WORKING HARMONIOUSLY WITH YOUR BOSS

Christopher Hegarty recommended several practical strategies on *How to Manage Your Boss* that are worthy of serious consideration.[4] If you plan to survive and thrive on the job, you should make an all-out attempt to establish an effective working relationship with your manager. Your boss has the position power, which is vested in her placement on the organizational chart, to grant or withhold a raise, continue or scratch a project, evaluate the quality of your work, and if necessary, discharge. Your manager's decisions have a direct bearing on your economic well-being and on your overall job satisfaction. For survival sake, you must learn to "manage your boss" so that she will grant you the permissions and resources that enable you to succeed.

You should consider it your number one priority to deal with your manager's perceptions. Right or wrong, your manager's opinions and feelings are real and must be dealt with as such. It does not really matter much whether you believe your boss to be fair, consistent, competent or worthwhile. The burden of proof is always on you to demonstrate your value and to make a measurable contribution to the organization. The burden is on you to shape the manager's attitude regarding the quality of your performance.

Below are several questions that you can ask yourself to determine how well you are managing your boss.

**1.** Do I play public win-lose games at my manager's expense? When I have some reservations about my manager's judgment, do I discuss the situation with her in a private, confidential setting? When I challenge my manager's decision and put forward new ideas, do I make these suggestions from a position of mutual trust and confidence? Or, is the relationship marked by competitiveness and one-upmanship?[5]

**2.** Do I provide face-saving for my manager when she makes a mistake? Am I out to make my boss look good? Am I prepared to help interpret or sell my manager's controversial stands on critical issues? Do I give her the benefit of the doubt?

**3.** Do I feed into co-workers' criticisms of my boss? Do I badmouth or gossip behind the scenes, or am I willing to say what I have to say directly to her? Do I also encourage my co-workers to speak openly with the boss?

**4.** In response to an unexpected criticism from the manager, do I keep my cool? Am I able to listen to her concerns without getting unduly defensive? Am I quick to search for alibis, or do I accept my responsibility if warranted? Do I dismiss as unimportant the mistake I made as if the manager is making too much of the situation, or do I accept her concern as legitimate and resolve to do better the next time?

**5.** Do I keep my manager informed as to what is happening on the job? Do I voluntarily share what is going well, roadblocks to success and suggestions for improving the overall operations of the organization? Does my manager find out from someone else about a mistake I made when I had the opportunity to apprise her of the situation beforehand? Do I fulfill my manager's "need to know," providing constant feedback, be it positive or negative?

**6.** Do I view my boss as a real human being possessing the limitations and insecurities associated with the rest of the human race?

**7.** Do I really understand the total complexity of my manager's job? Am I as sensitive to her job pressures as I expect her to be of mine?

**8.** Do I recognize and accept the legitimate authority of my boss to coach and counsel me, evaluate my work and hold me accountable?

**9.** When is the last time I gave my manager sincere, positive feedback?

**10.** When is the last time I volunteered to help my manager when an extra hand was needed?

**11.** Do I maximize my manager's strengths? Do I get her involved in my activities in which she is particularly talented or interested? Do I seek her advice in different situations?

**12.** When my best arguments and most compelling logic fail to convince the manager to accept my solution to a problem, do I keep hammering away hoping that she will give in? Do I bluff, threaten or pout to get my way? Or do I consider such losses a temporary set-back, not a total defeat, and try again later when the odds seem more favorable?

**13.** Am I truly self-motivated and self-disciplined to perform the job the best way I know how without the manager having to keep tabs on what I'm doing? Do I take pride in accomplishment and maintain a healthy self-image, or am I dependent on my manager's feedback to feel gratified on the job?

**14.** Are my expectations of others out of line? Do I expect my boss to always show appreciation for tasks well performed, that my co-workers should always be supportive and sensitive to my needs, that my job should always be interesting, meaningful or stimulating?

**15.** Have I thought through the reason I am on the payroll and the contribution I should be making? Do I understand and "buy into" the goals of my work area and organization? Do I take pride in being a member of my work team?

## Working With Your Manager's Decision-Making Style

Every boss prefers a certain type and amount of information in order to make important decisions. Observe your boss in action for a period of time and try to identify her unique decision-making style. It will help you influence her in the direction you desire. Here are four common styles that you can match to your boss.

### Management Style 1:

**Fact Finder** or *"Show Me The Evidence"*
If your manager is analytical and requires plenty of facts before making a decision, you should try to approach her with ample documentation to support your arguments. This may include statistics, charts or illustrations that will help "prove" your case. Highlight your presentation with objectivity, reason and analysis. Make certain you do your homework and can answer any pertinent questions or doubts that may be raised by your boss. Be organized. You simply can't "wing it" and be successful with this kind of manager.

### Management Style 2:

**Human Relater** or *"Who Will This Decision Help / Hurt?"*
Your boss might be the type who is very sensitive and supportive to those ideas that improve employee morale. She may be more concerned about people's feelings than she is about the facts. Indeed, productivity and quality of performance may not be her

chief concerns. If this is the case, you should pay attention to how a particular decision will affect worker satisfaction and employees' feelings of belonging to a team.

## Management Style 3:
### The Creative Genius *or "Is It Original?"*

Perhaps your boss has a strong need for creativity, innovation and imagination in her decision-making. She might rely on her intuitive skills and be willing to change plans in mid-stream. Her ideas may frequently result from sudden inspiration or insight. You should strive for originality in response to this management style. Develop ideas that are novel and eye-catching. Be "loose and free" and "go with the flow" to match your manager's spontaneity. And, because your manager is probably not the most organized person in the world, the burden is on you to be structured and orderly in your work.

## Management Style 4:
### Shaker & Mover *or "I Want Impact"*

If your boss is action-oriented, always talking about results and the "bottom-line," you should demonstrate the ability to develop practical and timely ideas that make a positive impact on the quantity and quality of work. Be particularly conscious of deadlines. Always try to stay one step ahead of your boss. Show that you are a self-starter and that you are totally committed to the job. Be prepared to sacrifice personal convenience and to work long, hard hours, because this style of manager will accept nothing less from you.

## Following Your Manager's Lead

When your manager gives you an assignment, does she expect you to "pick up the ball and run with it" until completion, or does she want you to include her in your plans every step of the way?

If you don't know, find out, and act in a manner that is supportive of her management style.

Is your boss a reader or a listener? A boss who shows a preference to read will consider your ideas only after she has had the chance to see them in writing. A boss who prefers to listen, on the other hand, will get frustrated by the written reports you submit and will respond more favorably if you first informally discuss the merits of your ideas. An effective employee is a flexible employee. On the job survival depends on your ability and willingness to work with and through your manager's particular style of decision making.

Are you upset when your boss does not ask you to contribute ideas and suggestions as part of her decision-making process? It is true that employees generally are more enthusiastic and able to implement a decision if they are allowed to have a say in making that decision. Often you are in the best position to know which policies and procedures are working and which ones need revision. You work with the problems and constraints of the job on a daily basis and can provide practical suggestions on how to overcome them.

Circumstances exist, however, when your manager simply cannot or should not allow you a direct say in the decision-making process. When these situations arise, it is important for you not to get unduly upset or antagonistic because your feelings are not being considered. Listed below are six occasions when your manager is justified in making unilateral decisions:

**1.** Your manager cannot afford the luxury of employee participation when quick and decisive action is required. Sometimes timeliness of action will make the difference between success and failure. If your manager postpones an important decision that requires immediate action because all employees want to be heard, she could be placing the organization in jeopardy. Procrastinating under the guise of participative management is a guarantee for employee frustration and failure.

**2.** When your manager's boss or someone representing a higher authority in the organization delivers a ruling, it is your manager's responsibility to communicate the decision and to ensure that it is implemented effectively. Your feelings, or those of the manager, regarding the wisdom of the decision take on secondary importance. Indeed, the manager could place her job security on the line if she openly criticizes the decision. Therefore, the only practical response to the situation may be to accept the ruling as a "given" and adjust to it.

**3.** Your manager would be wasting precious time if she allowed employees to get involved in a lengthy problem-solving discussion when there may exist a documented correct solution. The manager may have already investigated the matter and discovered, for example, that another organization has successfully handled the indentical situation. It would be folly in this case to re-invent the wheel. Full employee discussion on the subject could have the effect of diverting employees from more important tasks or arriving at an inferior decision based upon limited information.

**4.** When your manager feels very strongly about an issue that is less important to employees, it may be advantageous not to give her a hard time about it. She could become quite uncomfortable (if not resentful) if she allows herself to be changed by employee sentiment.

**5.** Your manager must literally ignore employee sentiment if the issue under consideration is governed by specific laws or regulations such as Equal Employment Opportunity Act, Worker's Compensation, Fair Labor Standards Act, or the Occupational Safety & Hazards Act. Your boss, as an agent of the organization, can unwittingly thrust your employer into a lengthy, expensive and exhaustive lawsuit as a result of attempting to satisfy majority opinion.

**6.** If the emotional maturity level of a number of co-workers leaves much to be desired, the manager will be too busy policing or disciplining and will have no patience left for group decision-making. Likewise, if many of your co-workers are new to the organization, they will require close supervision until they demonstrate the capacity to work independently and gain your manager's trust.

## Relating To Your New Manager

Perhaps a new boss has been hired to supervise your department. She doesn't know the quality of your work, and you are anxious to establish a good working relationship. What should you do?

Actions speak louder than words. Your most important objective at this time is to continue performing the job to the best of your ability. Your hard work will soon become evident to the new manager who will be very thankful for your independent initiative during this transitional period. Be sensitive to the new manager's needs as you would any new employee within your department. Your boss will require an orientation to the specific operating procedures, work routines, and social norms that make your department tick. She will need to know where to find things and identify who within the organization to contact when a particular problem arises. Your cooperation in helping her make sense out of the unfamiliar and to cut through the organization's red tape should pay off great dividends for you in the future.

Be patient with your new manager. She needs time to adjust to her new surroundings. She will make mistakes; don't judge her too harshly. Don't compare your new manager's supervisory style with that of her predecessor. One management style is not necessarily more effective than another, and employees who wish to establish an effective working relationship will simply have to adjust to the new manager's particular mode of behavior. Don't judge your new manager based upon what you have heard from employees who have previously worked for her. Your negative expectations could create a self-fulfilling prophecy and set you up for a poor working relationship.

Your new manager will not be impressed by attempts on your part to prejudice her against any of the co-workers with whom you have problems. Allow her to find out for herself the strengths and weaknesses of the employees within the department. Remember, your unsolicited criticism of others will be a negative reflection on you and will cause the manager to wonder if you are not some kind of agitator who thrives on departmental polarization and discord.

If fellow employees begin to bad-mouth your new manager and you haven't yet made up your mind about her, don't succumb to the pressure by joining them in the criticism. If you don't agree with your co-workers' negative sentiments, don't hesitate to say so. It's not necessary to debate with your colleagues in an attempt to change their minds; they are entitled to their opinions just as you are entitled to yours. When employees bad-mouth the manager, however, and expect you to join in, simply state, "I don't have that problem," or "I haven't experienced what you are talking about." Always try to encourage co-workers to address their problems directly with the manager instead of engaging in idle gossip and innuendo. It's the very best advice you could give them.

## If Your New Manager Is Promoted From Within The Department

You may have great difficulty appreciating the immense pressures of a person who is promoted into a management position from within her own department. While you may occasionally fantasize what it would be like to walk in the new manager's shoes, until you actually are given the responsibility, it is almost impossible for you to understand the burdens inherent in this position.

The manager who is promoted from within the ranks has particular challenges of establishing supervisory credibility. The manager's former peers are often resentful or jealous of her new status. They closely scrutinize her behavior and are quick to point out any signs that the manager has "changed" as a result of her position. Indeed, they often assign false motives to the new manager's actions, accusing her of being "power hungry" when she chooses to exercise some measure of control.

Of course, the relationship between the new manager and her former peers will never be the same. The new manager's responsibility for ensuring that the work gets done, to monitor, coach and counsel, evaluate performance, delegate and administer discipline irreversibly changes the nature of the relationship. Indeed, some new managers have great difficulty accepting the different status inherent in their roles. In their zeal not to be viewed as ogres, they attempt to establish a "one of the gang" or "good buddy" relationship with employees. They display a self-imposed impotence in an attempt to remain accepted or popular with fellow workers. However, most new managers soon resent this powerlessness and understand that a certain amount of control must be exercised. They quickly realize that their personal need for immediate popularity is of secondary importance to gaining employees' respect. They soon expect and require employee cooperation. They look to you for allegience and support.

# If Your Bid For A Promotion Has Been Rejected

Perhaps you just heard that someone else got the promotion that you deserved. Don't lose your cool and ruin your chances for future consideration. Ask for a consultation with your manager regarding what she considers to be your strengths and weaknesses relative to your potential for advancement. But remember, you asked for this feedback, so don't get defensive about any stated needs for improvement. Demonstrate an interest and willingness to participate in training development activities that will meet these professional developmental needs.

Above all, be very careful not to display an attitude of hostility or indignation for not getting the promotion. This attitude will probably come back to haunt you; there could be another promotional opportunity just around the corner, and your manager will be looking closely at your behavior to assess how you deal with disappointments or setbacks. Maintain your pride and self-esteem; look and act like a winner, even if you don't feel like one. How you behave at this time could make the difference in whether or not you will be seriously considered for promotion again.

# If Your Bid for Promotion is Accepted:
# A Special Challenge for The New Manager

If you've been recently promoted to management, you may have entered into a sort of hypnotic state characterized by exploding pride, idealism, and boundless energy. A pervasive head-in-the-clouds attitude may prevail, confident that managing employees will be a "piece of cake". You may be eager to experiment with an endless stream of new ideas for improving the department.

You may be anxious to make a positive impact, and to make an immediate imprint on how things will be run. In the process, you might assume unrealistic undertakings and move too quickly toward changes that are doomed to failure. This is because you may not yet have the capacity to wait and make reasonable plans based upon an accurate, realistic assessment of the department's needs.

If you're like many new managers, you may not recognize or acknowledge what is working well within your department or give enough credit to those employees who are effectively performing their jobs. Rather than take full advantage of the department's strengths, you are too consumed with correcting mistakes and filling voids. Single-handedly, you attempt to set things right; all decisions made by previous managers are suspect, and all employees seem to be called upon to justify their existence. In your obsession to change too much too soon, you make an indirect statement to employees that there must be something wrong with them. And, if the changes you promote are numerous, the work climate becomes unsettled, if not chaotic. Employees are traumatized by "change overload;" and they are thrust into states of paranoia and paralysis over the fear of losing their jobs.

As a new manager, try to demonstrate the capacity for patience and learn to live with the system for a while. Unless you are ordered by your boss to make immediate changes, your temporary acceptance of the status quo will buy you the time to learn what works and what doesn't. Your patience will also provide you with the opportunity to build credibility with employees. And when you finally decide to make the necessary changes to improve the department, you will be met with less employee resistance or hostility.

As a new manager, you may not like many of your supervisor's decisions or the arbitrary manner in which these decisions are made. Your employees may also be critical and are pressuring you to do something about it. This is commonly known as the "middle management squeeze."

Your challenge is to be an effective liaison or ombudsman as you market your employee's concerns. You will want to present feedback to your boss in a style that she will understand and appreciate. Don't always speak in terms of negative employee feelings or attitudes which your boss might consider irrelevant to her concerns. Don't approach the problem as a human relations issue unless you can equate employee attitudes with the bottom line.

Your responsibility is to provide evidence that the goals of your department are not being met because of poor quality employee relations. Try to demonstrate how employee morale is negatively affecting the self-interest of upper management. Symptoms may include: high turn-over costs in the form of expensive recruitment and training; payment for excessive short-term absences; payment of unnecessarry overtime because of duplication of effort; the potential for embarrassment or criticism as negative employee sentiment becomes evident to employees in other departments and company officials; reduction in the quality and quantity of work because employees don't completely understand their areas of responsibility and authority.

By attending to the self-interests of the boss in this fashion, you demonstrate that:

**1.** You are part of the management team

**2.** Your identification and loyalty are with upper management as well as with your employee group

**3.** You are sensitive to the fiscal needs of the organization.

And, if you are able to establish justification for a change in management practices based upon your boss's need to "look good," you make it easier for her to be sensitive to the needs of your employees.

# Notes

# Chapter 5

# HANDLING CRITICISM

You are judged not by your good intentions or how hard you try to do well but by the *results* you achieve and your *impact* upon others. This is an important concept to understand because you are probably in the least objective position to know how you come across to co-workers or how effective you are in performing your tasks. And, if you are like the rest of us, it is very tempting to justify or rationalize your behavior. It is all too easy to dismiss mistakes, discount errors in judgment, and sugarcoat bad news. In short, you may resist managerial feedback that reminds you of your inadequacies.

This practice of defending yourself against criticism is dangerous and it threatens your chances for job survival. If your boss is typical, she is very busy and cannot always find the time to provide you with daily performance feedback. You can easily "lull" yourself into a false sense of security, assuming that your work is satisfactory when, in fact, it is not. And, when the boss finally takes the time to inform you of any shortcomings in your performance, her feedback is both a shock and a bitter disappointment.

Don't delude yourself that "no news is good news" or that "it is better to leave well enough alone." What you don't know *can* hurt you, and a "head in the sand" attitude could lead to your demise on the job. Whether your manager is right or wrong in her perception, from her viewpoint, there is always a good reason to evaluate your work as she does. Her negative perceptions will not go away by ignoring them, and if you don't try to change these perceptions through words and deeds, her criticisms will become more severe. Therefore, act assertively in your own behalf; place yourself in a position to hear what's on your manager's mind and be certain to deal with her perceptions as a reality. Make it a point to initiate conversations with your boss on a periodic basis to find out where you stand. The information contained in the feedback you secure is critical for attaining job success.

## How to Ask For & Receive Feedback From Your Manager

Remember, your manager probably dislikes criticizing you as much as you dislike receiving criticism. In previous situations, however, your response to her negative feedback may have aggravated the working relationship. Without realizing it, you may have even "set up" your boss for confrontation by baiting and challenging her need for influence or control, thus questioning her authority to act as your manager. Now, because the manager *expects* you to be negative and resistant to change, she is more likely to have a defensive attitude when entering into discussions with you. Her need to dominate may become more important than to constructively communicate the specific performance issues that should be addressed. Therefore, your sincere interest in receiving feedback, whether positive or negative, will signify to the boss that you are now open to change and are prepared to take responsibility for the effect you have on others.

There are no guarantees that if you initiate a conversation with your boss to solicit feedback or clarify a misunderstanding you won't provoke a confrontation and jeopardize your job security. You may open a "can of worms." Perhaps once you start talking, you will say something that you don't mean (or really *do* mean) and regret it later. After all, you can never erase the spoken word. While your boss may not take immediate action, she will neither forget nor forgive what you may have said in anger.

Fear of getting angry or losing control can be overcome if you carefully plan for the feedback session. Listed below are a few pointers:

**1.** Limit the scope of the feedback session to one or two problem areas.

**2.** Demonstrate a willingness to recognize any limitations or need for change in yourself rather than pointing the finger of blame at your boss.

**3.** Ask plenty of questions to find out where your boss is "coming from." Avoid responding to her answers with "yes, but . . ." messages.

**4.** Display a self-disciplined communication style. Be deliberate and discreet in your choice of words, and also be aware of your non-verbal messages. (Eye contact, facial expression, overall posture, etc.)

**5.** If this is the first feedback session that you have initiated, consider it a first step in building a better working relationship. Your objective is not to win over the manager or to convince her that she's mistaken and you've been right all along. This approach will surely result in defensiveness on your manager's part. Rather, view this meeting as an information gathering session to gain a better understanding of your manager's point of view and specific expectations relating to your performance.

## How *Not* To Receive Feedback from Your Manager

On the following pages, you will find typical employee responses to criticism that often make managers more unreasonable or inflexible. To let you see the world through a manager's eyes, consider these 13 statements that have been made by managers when describing how some employees react to negative feedback:

**1.** "The employee doesn't give me a chance to talk. He argues with everything I have to say even before I have a chance to say it. He interrupts me constantly. I can't finish a sentence. He's contrary; if I say white, he says black. He uses the 'I, me, mine' statements, which indicate an 'I've got my mind made up' attitude. The discussion turns into a shouting match. I finally have to command him to be quiet! By this time, I'm anything but reasonable or objective. My comments have become much more extreme."

**2.** "The employee rarely looks at me when I talk to him. I don't know whether I'm being understood or if he's even listening. He doesn't take a personal interest in anything I'm saying. He seems withdrawn and distant. He's unwilling to reveal his own thoughts or get involved in the discussion. This infuriates me, and I sometimes think that's exactly what he wants. The lack of eye contact tells me that I don't have his attention or that his mind is somewhere else. His 'what's the big deal' attitude makes me believe he really doesn't care if I fire him. I know he needs the job, but if he maintains this attitude he'll force my hand."

**3.** "The employee actually starts to walk away from me before I'm finished talking to him, as if I'm keeping him from doing something more important. When I call him back, he returns acting as if he's doing me a favor. It's the ultimate in rudeness and smacks of insubordination. Rather than risk getting fired, he will always return and listen to what I'm saying, but with an expression that communicates, 'Say what you have to say, but make it fast.' He appears to be detached and unconcerned, and generally apathetic."

**4.** "The employee interjects humorous remarks even when I'm talking to him about a serious problem. He dismisses the importance of problems by actually laughing them off, saying things like, 'No harm done.' He'll try to side-track me and divert my attention to another matter as if the issue I'm addressing doesn't amount to much. What will it take to make him understand I'm serious?"

**5.** "After repeated attempts of explaining the procedure to him, the employee claims he doesn't understand how I want it done. He has had countless opportunities to request that I clarify my expectations, but he never asks. He simply will not admit when he lacks the skill or knowledge to do something. He would rather work with uncertainty and doubt and just plunge ahead, assuming that he's doing it right."

**6.** "The employee claims that the working conditions prevent him from accomplishing his tasks. If it's not one thing, it's another: the workload is too heavy; there is a lack of time/space/support staff/material; the temperature is not conducive to quality work; the procedures are not correct. He acts as if he is never responsible for the problem, and it's always someone or something else that needs to be improved. He shrugs off the notion that other co-workers are doing just fine with the same conditions. Or, he claims that somehow his situation is different, and I should be more sensitive to his particular needs."

**7.** "The employee feigns helplessness as if my expectations are always 'out of reach.' His response to my feedback amounts to a form of psychological blackmail. If I tell him he must try to work faster to meet production standards, he will say, 'Fine, if that's what you want, I'll do it, but don't blame me if my quality slips.' Or, if I tell him that he is making too many mistakes and to be more careful, his response is 'Fine, if that's what you want, I'll go slower but don't blame me if my production slips.' He acts as if I should not expect him to meet the same standards of quality and quantity that other employees are able to meet."

**8.** "The employee immediately tries to side-step the issue of what he did wrong by blaming it on my management style. He suggests that if I would only approach his mistakes in a different (more understanding) fashion, then these errors would not occur. He asks questions as if doubting what I say. He frequently responds to my questions with one of his own. I can never get a straight answer from him. Instead of concentrating on his mistake, I wind up defending myself. If I'm not careful, the employee controls the discussion by coaching and counseling *me* on how to be a more effective manager."

**9.** "The employee's first line of defense is to suggest that my criticism of his work is based on personal prejudice — that I don't like him; and because of this, I'm picking on him or treating him differently than the others. I do deal with co-workers' problems the same way, but I keep this confidential. A great deal of time and energy is spent assuring him that he is not a victim of discrimination. I sometimes think that he is using this as a means of making me feel guilty so I'll go softer on him."

**10.** "As soon as I'm finished giving the employee feedback behind closed doors and in a confidential setting, he goes directly to his co-workers and slants everything I said. He makes me sound like a real 'ogre.' He knows that I won't disclose to anyone what I said to him in confidence, and I really feel exploited by my self-imposed silence. Sooner or later the others will have his number, and he'll get no sympathy from me."

**11.** "The employee never does his dirty deeds in front of me. He always seems to wait until my day off or until I'm away from the department. Others report his shenanigans to me. When I approach him, his first response is to ask me who snitched. He concentrates on how others don't like him, are out to get him, and how I am always taking their side. He claims that he never starts an argument but somebody else always provokes him."

**12.** "The employee always acts like a martyr. He thinks I'm about to fire him whenever I give him the slightest feedback. He blows everything out of proportion and has a need to talk about how badly he needs his job because of his personal circumstances. He's overly friendly and eager to please. He enthusiastically agrees, even when there's no evidence that he really understands what I'm talking about. His unquestioning compliance seems more like a ploy to get me to forget about the problem and go about my business. But the overall effect is that he makes me question whether the problem will ever be corrected."

**13.** "The employee is always passive (like a puppy dog) when I criticize him. He takes it very personally, even if the matter I'm addressing is not a serious one. He asks if I want him to resign at the slightest provocation. I always seem to wind up assuring him that he is a good employee, not to take the criticism too hard, that the problem was not that important anyway. He routinely states that he's doing the best he can and that's all I can expect of him, yet the problem keeps recurring."

All of these employee responses signify resistance to a manager's feedback and suggest that the employee is not ready to listen or consider the manager's perception of what's wrong. Either the employee does not bother to listen at all, or he does pay attention but instantly rejects the message. The employee is either too busy defending, justifying, arguing, ignoring, or apologizing to hear the manager's feedback clearly and respond to it constructively. These responses lead the manager to one conclusion: 'I'm not getting through to this person, and I will have to use more extreme measures to get his attention.'

Instead of engaging in these various forms of defensive communication, you should try to talk with your manager in a direct and constructive manner. Be honest but also discreet. Your boss expects that you will be receptive to her feedback without necessarily groping for alibis; she expects that you will be prepared to readily answer questions or expects that you will state your case without theatrics or fanfare, to disagree but not become disagreeable. Above all, the manager expects that you *actively listen* to what she has to say.

# Accepting Criticism Responsibly

Regardless of the manager's criticism, there are six basic steps to follow when receiving specific negative feedback.

### Step 1: Actively Listen

When you are criticized by your manager because of a mistake, resist the strong temptation to immediately defend yourself. Your manager's first and most fundamental need when giving criticism is to know that you understand what she's saying and care about the problem she's addressing. She wants you to respect her viewpoint whether or not you agree. Only after you demonstrate an understanding of her message and show a sincere concern for the problem are you in a good position to present your side of the case.

Even if you think the manager's ideas are dead wrong, you must try to understand what she is experiencing or feeling. Acknowledge that she is acting on perceptions that are valid and real for her. Your first step in receiving criticism, therefore, is to initially "go along" with what your manager is saying rather than to block her message or change her opinion. When she realizes that she is being heard and understood, she is likely to be less defensive and her anger will be defused. She will be more willing to listen to you with an open ear.

## Step 2: Restatement

After you align with the manager's perceptions, demonstrate active listening by summarizing what you *thought* you heard the manager say: "Let me restate what I heard you say so that I'm sure I have it right. Are you saying this?" This is an effective means of checking for clear communication in a situation that calls for accuracy. If the manager gives you feedback to indicate that you did *not* hear her correctly, ask for more information to clarify the misunderstanding. Do not proceed any further until you have convinced her that you understand the criticism.

## Step 3: Request Additional Information

In addition to summarizing what you heard your manager say, consider inviting the boss to say more about her concerns: "Is there anything else I should know?" This request for additional information, however, must be sincere or you will be viewed by your manager as sarcastic and ridiculing.

Flush out what's on your manager's mind. Her words won't kill you. For survival's sake you must know where you stand with her and what specific expectations she has of you. How else will you know what you have to do differently to improve the working relationship?

As your manager is sharing the nature of her concern, closely follow her thoughts and align with her perceptions. By getting actively involved with what she is saying you can gain valuable insight into the assumptions she is making and learn *why* she is so upset. Furthermore, when she senses that you are not fighting her, she may let her guard down, and then you are in a pivotal position to influence her attitude and behavior.

## Step 4: Present Your Position

Only after you have confirmed your understanding of the manager's criticism and have aligned with her concerns, should you advance your own point of view. Ask the manager if she has overlooked any particular details. Try to complete the picture for your manager describing what actually happened. Present your case objectively and unemotionally. Use whatever facts are available to support your statements.

If appropriate, don't hesitate to admit where you were wrong, and don't try to set up an alibi or dismiss the importance of your errors. When you admit a mistake that you made, your manager will respect you for taking responsibility for your actions, and she may be more willing to admit where she was mistaken. If you attempt to 'stonewall' any possibility for personal wrongdoing, however, your manager will be more inflexible in her attitudes and harsh in her judgment.

## Step 5: Know When To Stop

If the manager rejects your best arguments, stop trying to defend yourself and don't repeat the same story over and over in hopes that she will finally see the light. If you reach a certain point in the discussion when neither you nor the manager is learning anything new from the exchange, try to end the conversation gracefully. If possible, identify and summarize the areas of agreement and the remaining differences of opinion. Temporarily 'agree to disagree.' Communicate to your manager that you understand her specific expectations and will commit yourself to meeting them.

## Step 6: Analyze What Happened

After the meeting has ended, try to assess the nature and extent of the disagreement. Avoid private thoughts such as: *"I'm being dumped on again. . . How much more of this can I take. . . I really don't need this kind of aggravation. . . Maybe it's time to quit. . . But why should I take this sitting down. . . I've got to continue my efforts to prove her wrong."*[6] Remember, if you view yourself as a victim and a captive in the situation, you are likely to provoke defensive responses from the manager.

Rather than blame your manager or continue your efforts to change her thinking, place the specific incident behind you and look to the future. Try to diagnose possible causes of the conflict:

- Your manager may simply see the world differently than you do because of her particular background and experiences.

- She may have a different set of priorities.

- Perhaps you were not sure of her specific expectations in the first place.

- The manager's boss may be leaning on her to act in a particular manner in relation to all employees. (If this is the case, your manager is probably adament in her perspective because *her* job survival is at stake.)

- You and the manager may be equally committed to the success of the organization but are using different methods of achieving this goal.

As you try to understand the underlying causes of the disagreement, do not use these differences of perspective as an excuse for giving less than 100% on the job. Most working relationships can succeed even if significant differences exist, providing both persons accept each other as professionals with a task to perform and recognize that they are truly dependent upon one another for success on the job.

# Notes

# Chapter 6

# MANAGING CONFLICT
# WITH CO-WORKERS

Your manager dislikes having employees constantly bickering with each other; it simply takes time and energy away from the important tasks that must be completed. Furthermore, she probably resents having to play the role of judge and jury over employee disputes. In most cases, she isn't present to see for herself who started the conflict and therefore, she lacks the first-hand knowledge to assess responsibility. She does not want to be 'nickeled and dimed' by employee discord and expects that you are adult enough to handle such conflicts in an independent fashion.

If your goal is to get the job done with maximum effectiveness and satisfaction, you should learn how to independently manage interpersonal conflicts. This challenge is always difficult because co-workers are constantly placing demands upon you. On occasion, they may question your honesty, impugn your integrity, doubt your motives, challenge your information and test your patience. They may do any or all of these things in a demanding or hostile manner. And of course, in order to save face, the temptation is great to respond with personal defensiveness.

It may be easier for you to maintain composure under such circumstances if you understand a little more about the nature of
conflict. Let's explore three myths.

## Myth #1:
### Conflict is, by its very nature, counter-productive.

Actually, conflict is neither good nor bad; conflict just is! How you
*deal* with conflict, however, can be very positive or negative and
can either escalate a problem or defuse it. Your response to any
conflict can be either constructive or defensive-inducing and
counter productive.

The myth that conflict is inherently negative may cause you to
assume that there's something wrong with either you or a co-
worker if you can't reach agreement. This assumption is
erroneous. To demand that a co-worker think or act like you do
stifles creativity and prevents the open exploration and exchange
of information that helps you grow. You should learn to
acknowledge and respect differing points of view. Through the
marketplace of competing ideas, you can choose what's right for
you. View conflict as an opportunity to test your beliefs and
adjust to different styles of behavior. Don't deny a conflict when
it exists or attempt to artificially smooth it over. Confront and
learn from it.

## Myth #2:
### Conflict is caused by someone out to make trouble.

Few employees engaged in conflict actually *intend* to be destructive or counter-productive. Each is striving to have a need met,
and achieve some positive outcome (at least from his own
perspective). The damage done to someone else is either ac-
cidental or seen as necessary to achieve a personal objective.
Give your co-worker the benefit of the doubt by assuming that his
motives are pure, and by providing him with an opportunity to
save face when his actions inconvenience or irritate you. To
suggest that his behavior is premeditated and malicious only

serves to aggravate the situation and will create a negative "self-fulfilling prophesy."

## Myth #3:
### *In order to work effectively with someone, I have to like him.*

Perhaps this is the most common and dangerous myth of all. Liking a co-worker on a personal level makes it easier to work with him, but disliking him does not preclude the necessity for cooperation. As a professional, you have a specific role to play, procedures to follow, and goals to achieve. You cannot afford to subvert the mission of the organization because of a personality difference. To do so is the ultimate cop-out. As a member of a working team, your task accomplishment depends upon the success of co-workers. And, regardless of your feelings toward someone, a good working relationship at least keeps the results channels greased for when you will need them.

If you accept these three myths about conflict as reality, you will often find yourself in win-lose confrontations with your co-workers. You will see problems only from your own point of view, and you will not recognize that your goals and your co-workers' goals are *both* important. In your effort to dominate, you will resort to a variety of counter-productive activities resulting in a breakdown of communication, distrust, fear and aggression.

Although you may occasionally win over the objections of your co-worker and gain some measure of immediate gratification, it will be a short-lived victory. The co-worker, harboring resentment over his loss, will renew the battle when you are in a weaker position. Or, he will simply cut off communications and withhold valuable information which you may need to succeed on the job. Neither response is desirable.

To survive on the job you need to know that:

1. It is better to cooperate than to dominate. Attempts at

resolving a conflict reap greater results than efforts to defeat a co-worker.

2. Differences of opinion with a co-worker are okay as long as you respect his point of view and can find enough common ground to work cooperatively.

3. Personalizing the issue by attacking a co-worker when he disagrees with you is *not* okay. It blocks communication and escalates the conflict.

If you are having trouble securing cooperation from a co-worker, you may be demonstrating a rather limited set of persuasive strategies to turn the situation around. Ironically, your failure may be the result of believing in and practicing the famous Golden Rule principle: "Do unto others as *you would have others do unto you.*" The Golden Rule principle has a limited value in resolving conflict because it is effective only when the co-worker is like you and has similar preferences, needs and expectations. The Golden Rule principle might be more effective if it read: "Do unto others *as they would like to be treated;*" this would highlight your responsibility to meet *their* needs and expectations, even if these may differ from your own.[6]

Always reduce the co-worker's excuses for being your adversary by communicating to him that you're not out to inconvenience, embarrass or harm him. But, also let him know that you won't allow him to inconvenience, embarrass, or harm you, and that *you* also have needs and expectations to meet. This mutual respect for one another's potential to be an ally or a foe will maximize your chances for securing cooperation.

## Practicing Empathy

It's easy to point the finger of blame, shame, guilt and responsibility at a co-worker when a working relationship has gone sour. But you can never break the wall of animosity by scapegoating. Your success in achieving a more effective working relationship depends upon your ability to empathize. When you engage in empathy you:

1. Suspend your judgment of the co-worker just long enough to see the world through his eyes.

2 . Sense the co-worker's confusion, timidity, suspicion, anger, or feelings of being treated unfairly, as if they were your own.

3. Appreciate that no matter how unreasonable, irrational or immoral the co-worker's behavior may appear to you, it is quite reasonable, rational and moral to the co-worker.

4. Reflect upon how the co-worker has responded to past behaviors on your part.

5. Predict how he might act in the future based upon what you might say or do.

6. Choose to act in a manner that you think will evoke the most positive responses in the co-worker.

Unfortunately, when co-workers are in conflict, neither party is inclined to practice empathy. Instead, most employees offer an *evaluative* understanding, such as, "I understand what is wrong with you." Or they rest their hopes for a cooperative working relationship on the other person changing *his* attitude or behavior. Empathic understanding, on the other hand, is non-evaluative understanding. William Haney, in his book, *Communication and Organizational Behavior*, gives an example:

*"Assuming you are Mr. A, and you have tried in vain to convince Mr. B of an idea or proposal, and Mr. B, his defenses thoroughly aroused, doggedly resists. It does no good for you to continue to shout and pound the table. What you must do is something entirely different, namely, temporarily suspend your purposes*

*and listen to Mr. B and listen non-evaluatively. Such listening means listening without argument or passing judgment, listening fully in order to understand thoroughly how the problem looks to Mr. B and why Mr. B's resistance make sense to him, given the kind of and amount of information he possesses, given the goals for which he is striving.*

*What happens to Mr. B if you listen non-evaulatively to him is that, no longer confronted with the necessity of countering your arguments, he begins to relax the rigidity of his defenses. His defensive utterances give way to informative utterances. He begins to tone down the absoluteness of his statements, to be less stereotyped and propagandistic in his responses.*

*Communication being a process of interaction, something also begins to happen to you. Because Mr. B is making less extreme statements, you relax. Having entered empathically into his view of the world, you may succeed in coming to the conclusion that his views, while still unacceptable, at least make a certain amount of sense, given his assumptions."*[7]

When you are open to the way life works as experienced by a co-worker, when you can take his world and place it into your own framework (even at the risk of changing your own perceptions), it is the turning point in the conflict. It is the point at which you begin to acknowledge that the co-worker is neither dishonest nor insane, but merely different as a result of his experiences.

You will feel more secure in a working relationship when you can interpret correctly the attitudes and intentions of a co-worker, perceive situations from his viewpoint, and anticipate his behavior in various situations. Your ability to accurately predict the co-workers responses to what you may say or do enables you to avoid unnecessary friction.

On the other hand, if you lack this empathic ability, you cannot trust your skills in dealing with the co-worker and you are compelled to be on guard and reactive in the relationship. A state of mutual threat between you and the co-worker results in a communication deadlock. Stereotypes are created and false intentions are attributed. Defensive measures on the one side confirm any fears on the other side, and by acting in a manner that validates your co-worker's worst fears, you move toward a confrontation that perhaps neither of you really wants. Once this vicious cycle is firmly established, it becomes difficult to break. The threat perceived on both sides prevents or distorts communication. This stand-off often breeds habitual resentment and stubbornness. The controlling anger results in general irritability and always has the potential of becoming explosive. The end result: you cooperate as little as possible and only when absolutely necessary to get the job done. Sometimes the job just *doesn't* get done.

You can take the first step to improve a working relationship without waiting for signs that the co-worker is willing or ready to change. After all, it takes only one person to break the ice. The dropping of some defensiveness on your part could lead to a dropping of defensiveness by the co-worker. But don't look for immediate results. Your overtures of goodwill are likely to be met initially with surprise and suspicion. Over time, however, your sincere and consistent willingness to cooperate should pay off.

## Independent Exercise to Resolve Co-worker Conflict

You can implement the following conflict-resolution procedure without requiring assistance from your boss or consent of the co-worker. It is advantageous, of course, for the co-worker to be a willing partner in the exercise, but it's not necessary to achieve positive results. In fact, your ability to take independent action, regardless of the co-worker's inclination to do likewise, is the value of this exercise.

## Step 1:
### *Develop A List Of the Co-Worker's Good Qualities*

Recognize and acknowledge what the co-worker is doing right. What behaviors do you observe in the co-worker that you appreciate and wish to continue? Unfortunately, when a working relationship has gone sour, you have a tendency to overlook (or take for granted) these positive qualities in a person. But, you run the risk of extinguishing those behaviors you appreciate in a co-worker when you choose to ignore them. Good behavior needs reinforcement. The co-worker needs to know that you notice when he's doing things to make your job easier, more satisfying, or more effective. Therefore, the first step in resolving the conflict is to develop a laundry list of what the co-worker is doing right.

## Step 2:
### *Develop A List of Your Bad Habits*

Consider what you have done in the past to provoke the co-worker. Recall his complaints or requests for change on your part. Then develop a laundry list of what you do too much or too little of that probably frustrates the co-worker. If you're not certain how to complete this list, place yourself in the co-worker's shoes; what would *he* say you do too much or too little of that frustrates him? It doesn't matter whether the co-worker is right or wrong or whether you do these things intentionally. If he might perceive that you do too much or too little of something, include it in this list.

## Step 3:
### *Develop Commitments For Behavioral Change*

Review your list of bad habits (as perceived by the co-worker) and determine which behaviors you are willing to change to improve the working relationship. Write down three things that you're going to do more or less of that will increase your chances for cooperation with the co-worker. Be certain that you commit to things that you are *willing* and *able* to accomplish within a reasonable time-frame. Also, make certain that your three commitments for change will be *observable* to the co-worker. It's not enough to state, for example, that "I will improve my attitude" or that "I will take more initiative to help you." What will you do specifically to improve your attitude or to demonstrate greater initiative? In other words, describe your commitments in behavioral terms.

## Step 4:
### *Initiate A Meeting With the Co-Worker to Share Your Information*

After you have completed the previous steps, it is important for you to initiate a confidential meeting with the co-worker to explain the thought processes you've gone through and share your information. It is entirely possible that the co-worker will be just a little bit stunned and suspicious of this whole process. Anticipate and plan for potential resistance, and be determined that regardless of the co-worker's response, you will remain positive. Don't get upset or give up even if the co-worker demonstrates a defensive posture throughout the duration of the meeting. Remember, the co-worker cannot make you act defensively or hostile; you are responsible for your own behavior.

Continuously ask for feedback from the co-worker as you share the information contained in your three lists. Solicit his ideas, check for clear communication, and align yourself with his thoughts. It is particularly important for you not to get angry if he readily agrees with everything you mentioned on your second list (those things you do that bother him). His agreement simply shows that you were successful in seeing the world though his eyes.

When you divulge your list of commitments, ask the co-worker to accept these behavioral changes as good faith gestures to improve the working relationship. If necessary, be prepared to develop new commitments based upon the co-worker's feedback. State that you intend to act immediately on these behavioral change commitments, and request that the co-worker give you constructive feedback when he observes you are not living up to them.

Your efforts will be wasted if you do not deliver on your commitments to improve the working relationship. Even if the co-worker does not choose to offer commitments of his own to improve the relationship, you have accomplished three things by engaging in this exercise:

1. You have become more introspective regarding your behavior and its effect upon the co-worker.

2. You have made it easier for the co-worker to change by demonstrating a willingness to first change yourself.

3. You have done your part to break the deadlock by acting responsibily. The ball is now in your co-worker's court to respond in kind.

## Additional Conflict Resolution Procedures

If you can encourage a fellow worker to engage in a conflict resolution procedure with you, the following are additional exercises that can assist in overcoming your differences. Each exercise is based on the simple principle that sometimes you have to give in order to get.

### Letter Exercise

### Step 1:
Write a letter to one another, divided into the following parts:

*I believe that you could do your job better, easier, or in a more satisfying manner if I would **stop** doing the following things. . .*

*I believe that you could do your job better, easier, or in a more satisfying manner if I would* **start** *doing the following things...*

*I could do my job better, easier, or in a more satisfying manner if you would* **stop** *doing the following things...*

*I could do my job better, easier, or in a more satisfying manner if you would* **start** *doing the following things...*

**Step 2:**

Meet with one another to share your respective letters. Compare and contrast the information contained in these letters and "negotiate" the giving and receiving of commitments to one another. Make sure you advance commitments that you can honor and that will make a positive difference in the co-worker's job effectiveness or satisfaction. Agree to provide each other with immediate (constructive) feedback when you observe the other successfully honoring or reneging on the commitments made. Arrange a follow-up meeting to evaluate how successfully each of you has delivered on your commitments.

## Job Analysis Exercise

Engage in a dialogue with the co-worker and try to arrive at a mutual understanding regarding "What are we here to accomplish?" (Goals): "Who is responsible for completing the various tasks?" (Roles): "How are we supposed to perform these tasks?" (Procedures)

You will know your dialogue has been successful if you can agree on the answers for the following additional questions under each heading:

**Goals:** "What is the purpose of our organization/department? Why do our specific jobs exist? Who are our clients?" Include in your discussion fellow employees within and outside your department as well as customers. "What damage is done when we don't cooperate or don't carry out our responsibilities in an effective manner?"

**Roles:** "In what ways are we interdependent upon one another? For example, in what ways do you depend on me for your successful completion of tasks and vise-versa? Where do my responsibilities begin and end, and when do they overlap with yours."

**Procedures:** "What written procedures exist that describe the way we're supposed to work? Are these procedures up to date? Relevant? Are we following the procedures? Can we revise them so they meet our mutual goals?"

Determine individual commitments for behavioral change by asking yourselves one additional question: "What specific things can we do to help each other succeed and be satisfied in our jobs?" Arrange for a follow-up meeting to assess whether or not you both honored these commitments. Agree to give each other constructive feedback whenever appropriate.

### Needs Analysis Exercise

Each of you complete the Cooperation Chart on the following page. Your objective is to develop new ways to better meet each other's needs, expectations and hopes on the job. As with the preceding exercises, meet with the co-worker to compare and contrast information as contained in the charts. Negotiate commitments and a timetable for completion of the expected performance. Establish a method for evaluation and a feedback process to monitor and reinforce your progress.

# COOPERATION CHART

What are the co-worker's needs, expectations, and hopes of me so that he can do his job in an effective and satisfying manner?

---

Co-worker's needs and expectations that *are* being met.

---

Co-worker's needs and expectations that *are not* being met.

---

Significant and workable commitments (no more than 3) that I will make based on this assessment.

---

Timetable for completion of expected performance (to be exhibited by what date).

---

## Providing Positive Feedback

It is important that you learn to notice and acknowledge that the co-worker is doing something right. Try to be frequent in providing positive feedback to the co-worker as long as you're sincere about it. Timeliness of feedback is also important: deliver the compliment immediately following an event that is worthy of praise. Pleasantly surprise the co-worker by providing positive feedback when he least expects it or when others can overhear it. In these ways your compliments will have greater value. Be specific when you deliver a compliment by describing exactly what the co-worker did to earn your praise. Simply state what you saw or heard and describe the positive effect this behavior had upon you. But, when you decide to offer praise, don't give the co-worker double messages by adding what he could have done differently or better: *"That was great! Now if only you could have..."* *"You did well, but..."* The co-worker is sure to walk away from the interaction dwelling on the negative part of the feedback and the compliment will have lost its effect.

## Providing Constructive Criticism

When you have to give criticism to a co-worker, the burden is on you to be both constructive and informative in your feedback. You want to provide the criticism in a manner that minimizes defensiveness and enables the co-worker to actually learn from your feedback. The following suggestions might prove helpful:

**1.** Provide criticism immediately following an event that is worthy of comment providing you are able to remain calm and maintain self-control. Try to delay the negative feedback if either you or the co-worker are angry, hurt or frustrated. Wait until things cool down before you approach the matter. But don't wait too long because you or the co-worker might forget specifically what happened, distort important aspects of the incident, or even deny that the event took place.

**2.** Do not deliver criticism in front of others. The co-worker will not readily admit responsibility for his actions, and he will likely attack you because there is no opportunity to save face. Embarrassing and ridiculing a co-worker or making an example of him will only result in an ugly confrontation that neither of you want.

**3.** Limit your criticism to one subject at a time. Don't accumulate a long list of complaints against the co-worker and bombard him with a barrage of negative feedback. The co-worker will have every reason to conclude that a) you don't like him, b) there is nothing he can do to please you or c) the situation is hopeless.

**4.** If you have worked with someone for a period of time, you know what things to say or do to provoke him; you know what he is sensitive about and have the power to embarrass or ignite his emotions. Regardless of any temptation, it is always better to hold some things back, that is, don't hit below the belt or unleash your most stinging criticism to disarm him. You may satisfy your immediate need to get even, win or dominate, but by being brutally honest with your co-worker, you risk irreversibly damaging the relationship.

**5.** Be specific in your criticism by simply describing what the co-worker did or said and its negative effect on you. Be certain to address the behavior and not attack the person displaying the behavior. Don't judge his actions by suggesting that what he did was wrong, stupid or inconsiderate. Don't question his motives or impugn his integrity. Give him the benefit of the doubt that he didn't intentionally act in a particular manner to hurt or inconvenience you. Simply focus on the negative impact that his behavior had on you.

**6.** Try to describe for the co-worker what you would appreciate him doing differently and the positive impact this behavior would have on you. Before you make such a request, consider what you can do to make it easier for the co-worker to change in the direction you desire.

Immediately deliver a compliment if the co-worker makes a positive effort to change his behavior. By showing appreciation for even small gestures of good faith, you reinforce the co-worker's willingness to cooperate. On the other hand, if you ignore or take for granted the co-worker's positive actions, you risk extinguishing his willingness to be a resource and an ally.

## Avoiding Gossip

The surest way of violating a co-worker's trust is to bad-mouth him behind his back or divulge information that he has given you in confidence. Gossip is cheap and shallow talk that is rarely grounded in fact. It can, however, be very personally or professionally damaging to the employee who is the subject of such talk. Sometimes the content of gossip is titillating, and it is very tempting to pass the message on (confidentially) to the next person. This activity, although usually pursued without malicious intent, is both insensitive and irresponsible.

If you are busy on important tasks, you don't have time for such idle gossip. You're simply too busy pursuing the day to day operations of your job. If you happen to be the recipient of gossip, however, you should label it as such and extinguish the conversation by not feeding into it. You can avoid gossip by making a habit of talking openly and honestly to those employees with whom your experiencing a difficulty. Address no one else regarding these issues unless you believe that there is a bonafide job related reason for another person to know. Encourage co-workers to also talk directly and candidly with one another.

Never pass information along unless you are convinced that you can "stand behind" what you say. When you do have something of importance to communicate to others, your remarks will be taken more seriously. Others will turn to you for advice on both professional and personal matters because they trust that the information they give you will be held in the strictest confidence. By avoiding gossip, you will be an employee who enjoys credibility and respect; you will be valued as a trusted colleague who others can turn to when the need arises.

# Notes

# Chapter 7

# HOW TO LOSE SUPPORT AND ALIENATE PEOPLE

Let's assume for the moment that you have just received some stinging criticism from your manager. In your opinion, the criticism is unjustified. You view yourself as a victim of managerial abuse. You are angry. You also feel somewhat powerless and captive to your situation: *"Look what she's done to me now. I've done my best but nothing ever seems to please her. She's really got me in trouble this time. But she's not going to get away with it."*

Your main desire is to deny the legitimacy of the criticism and to fight back. You want everyone to know that your manager is incompetent and unfair. Your secret hope is that she will be punished for "managerial malpractice" and will be removed from her position.

You take some satisfaction in thinking that you're not alone in your dislike for the manager: *"I'm not the only one who gets this kind of treatment. Everyone in the department feels the same way about her. You should hear our conversations at lunch. Somebody really should step in and straighten her out, or we're all going to quit."*

Your statements reflect a need to depersonalize the criticism, to demonstrate that it is not simply a personal concern, and that the magnitude of the problem warrants an investigation into the manager's competency. You try to shift the focus of attention away from your behavior and rebuff criticism lodged against you by discrediting the manager who is the source of criticism.

You spend a significant amount of time justifying your performance. You want to be absolved of any wrongdoing and be vindicated for your actions: *"Now that you've heard my side and understand what really happened, don't you think I did the right thing? What else could I have done under the circumstances? If you were my manager, you wouldn't have done this to me!"*

You are slow to admit any responsibility for provoking the manager. You repel any suggestion to meet the manager halfway or to demonstrate a willingness to change based upon the manager's feedback. Perhaps you are still too hurt or embarrassed by the criticism. You are fearful that any initiative on your part to improve the working relationship would be interpreted as a sign of weakness or an admission of guilt: *"Why is it always me that has to change to please her? She's wrong and everyone knows it. I'm not going to be the one who backs down this time. She's at fault and will have to make the first move."*

If the above examples reflect your typical response to negative feedback, you are probably embarked on a collision course with your manager. A polarization may exist between you and your boss that is marked by communication breakdown, resentment, distrust and fear. It is a manager-employee relationship that will lead to confrontation and ultimately result in termination. Without realizing it, you may be exhibiting behavior that is alienating to your boss and co-workers. Your continuous griping and dumping, agitating manner, and dogmatic approach to addressing problems, may result in your losing the necessary support of others to survive on the job.

# The Gripe and Dumper

You may be a gripe and dumper without knowing it. If you are a gripe and dumper, you rarely take any responsibility for a problem or offer any solutions that include change on your part. Instead, you are too obsessed with who started the problem or who is to blame. You are too busy judging the motivation or behavior of others, and too overwhelmed by feelings of being victimized to be a constructive team player.

As a gripe and dumper, you might be absolutely correct in identifying a problem or calling attention to a particular job condition that makes your work more difficult. Your motivation may be pure, but your style in addressing the issue is such a turn-off that the manager sees *you* as the problem: *"Anybody with brains can tell you that this procedure is stupid. . . The longer I work here the more I realize that I'm the only one who cares enough to complain. . . I don't know about you but I take my job seriously. . . Unfortunately, I don't have the authority to change things around here: I just take orders, I don't give them. Our boss should know enough, or at least have the courage to solve this problem. But obviously she doesn't care or is too busy looking out for herself."* Your manager, who overhears and resents these remarks, correctly believes that you're contributing to the department's unrest; she interprets your language as inflammatory and devisive and naturally perceives you as a threat to her managerial security.

If you are a gripe and dumper you probably have unrealistic expectations of the time it takes to solve a problem. Because of your need for immediate gratification, you advance simplistic, quick-fix remedies to complex issues: *"She's been working on those revisions for weeks now. It will take forever before she finishes. We all know what needs to be done. Let's just do it and work out the bugs as we go along. Anything is better than this!"*

Your lack of patience and understanding for others' work needs, therefore, causes co-workers to secretly view you as spoiled or self-centered.

You take for granted what's good about your job, and you are obsessed with everything that's wrong, causing you to display an overall negative attitude. You repel constructive attempts by the boss and your co-workers to deal with problems. You throw cold water on their solutions, dismissing their ideas as unworkable, impractical or undesirable. You oppose others beyond reason and exaggerate differences of opinions: *"How can you say things are getting better? Are you really satisfied with her answers? Can't you see that she's just throwing us a bone so we'll stop complaining? The longer this goes on, the worse it's going to get."*

You may be alienating yourself from your job and co-workers: *"I don't like it here;" "I'd rather be somewhere else;" "I don't like either the job or the co-workers with whom I have contact;" "I don't even like myself within this situation."* As if not content to be miserable alone, you remind others about how bad things are. You exaggerate minor problems into major catastrophes and dramatize colleague's mistakes. In short, you agitate people and aggravate problems.

## The Agitator

An agitator is a worker who is titillated by rumor and innuendo. If you are an agitator, you pick on or taunt others. You may even find satisfaction in a certain worker's misfortune or do your part in subtle ways to create trouble for him. You are unable to handle disagreement. Rather than argue the merits of a particular opinion, you attack the person presenting a different point of view: *"If I were you, I wouldn't be so judgmental. . . You don't know everything there is to know. . . I'm not the only one who thinks you're wrong. . . You would say something like that. . . That may work for you, but what about the rest of us?"*

When you confront co-workers, you yell, interrupt, bait, blame, shame and scapegoat them: *"That's the dumbest thing I've ever heard. . . You've got to be kidding. . . That's a laugh."* You walk away from a discussion before it's completed, leaving your co-workers frustrated and furious.

Your statements often have double meanings. It is not what you say that has impact as much as how you say it. Your compliments (however few) are backhanded: *"It doesn't look bad for a first try. . . Your idea might help. But, of course, anything would be better than what we have now. . . That might work, but it's not the first time I've heard the suggestion. . . You're not doing bad for just starting out. It takes time to know as much as I do. . . You did okay, considering the amount of time you put into it."*

If you are an agitator, you practice subtle forms of sabotage and manipulation. You go around or above people to gain satisfaction. You talk behind a co-worker's back to inconvenience, embarrass or block his progress. During department meetings, when you're given an opportunity to openly voice concerns or suggest ways to improve the working environment, you are curiously silent. But *after* the meeting is over, you engage in animated discussions lamenting how bad things are at work: *"Do you believe we spent an hour at that meeting and we didn't solve any of our problems. . . what a waste of time. . . What was decided will never work. . . I don't know about you, but I think we're getting a raw deal."*

With the instincts of a guerrilla fighter, you are the catalyst for intergroup conflict within the department. You thrive on division among employees and frequently play both ends against the middle. You are tantalized by employee discord and are eager to stir things up to make your work more interesting: *"They always get everthing they want. Nobody cares about us. How come we always have to help them? We do our part, why can't they? We're the only ones that seem to really be working around here. Do you think they're worth the money they get paid? I wonder what they've got on the boss to always pull the soft jobs."*

As an agitator, you often resist and reject your manager's leadership. You believe that someone else (perhaps you) could perform the management functions more effectively. You have serious problems taking directions, and you have a gut level need to constantly second-guess the manager's decisions: *"This manager thinks she's a hot shot. . . I could do her job blind-folded. . . Who is she to tell me how to do this job. She's never done it!"*

As an agitator, you ignore the manager's strengths and constantly publicize her flaws. You believe her to be an unnecessary burden and a meddler into your affairs. You display a prima donna attitude, always preferring to do things your way. You often see yourself as the exception to the rule and frequently argue that your situation is different from the others: *"That solution may work for everyone else, but what about me?"* You display an attitude that, "My way of looking at the problem is the only correct way," and therefore you can correctly be labeled a dogmatist.

## The Dogmatist

A dogmatist is an employee who divides co-workers into two camps: the "good," "intelligent," and "correct" people versus the "bad," "ignorant," and "misguided" people. Of course, the dogmatist views himself firmly entrenched in the first camp, and anyone who disagrees with him is hopelessly lodged in the second camp. If you are a dogmatist, you sincerely believe that 1) you have a corner on truth, 2) your window to the world is the most clear and least distorted, 3) your path is the truest. You are likely to talk to others in a condescending manner as if they are children needing a lecture: *"I've been doing this job longer than most of you, and I'm telling you that this is the only way it can be done. . . . Those of you who think otherwise have really got your head in the sand."*

As a dogmatist, your relationship with co-workers is strong and secure as long as they agree with you; if they believe and behave the way you do, they have earned your friendship and everything is peachy. But, when your boss or co-workers don't think or act in a manner that you agree with, you view this as a personal rejection and they become your enemies: *"I thought you were my friend...I'm really surprised that you're opposing me on this...How can we work together if this is how you feel?"*

If you're a gripe and dumper, agitator or dogmatist, you will lose support and alienate co-workers because of your overall negative attitude. You will destroy the relationship with your boss, in particular, by not legitimizing her authority. Keep in mind that you don't have to be blatantly insubordinate to lose your job. There are more subtle, yet damaging, ways to erode your credibility and destroy your manager's confidence in you. For example, don't test your manager's patience by feigning:

1. Misunderstanding: *"That's not what I understood you to say."*

2. Memory lapse: *"I forgot."*

3. Helplessness: *"I'm already overloaded and I don't have the time to do it right now."*

4. Paralysis: *"I've always done it this way. I've tried that before, but it didn't work for me."*

If the responses described in this chapter ring all too true, your behavior on the job is counter-productive, destructive and self-defeating. Remember, it may not matter whether you are accomplishing your tasks in a competent manner. If the quality of your employee relations is unacceptable, the manager will begin to document how your attitude negatively affects co-workers' performance. She will elaborate on the waste of time and energy expended to "keep a lid" on your defensiveness. She will build a case that supports the need for your involuntary discharge, or she will try to get you to resign by making your life on the job miserable. But don't blame the manager; the negative behavior you displayed at work may have provoked your own rejection.

# Notes

# Chapter 8

# HOW TO WIN SUPPORT AND INFLUENCE PEOPLE

If you are to survive on the job, you must learn how to win support and influence people within your organization. To accomplish this goal, you should:

1. Demonstrate intimate knowledge of all your job responsibilities, and perform your tasks in a consistently skillful manner

2. Exhibit high character and personal integrity in all of your working relationships

3. Exercise a sense of good will and allegiance to your employer, department, manager and co-workers

## Know Your Job Responsibilities And Skillfully Perform Them

Your professional credibility depends upon how well you understand your manager's expectations regarding the task to be accomplished, the results to be achieved, and the methods by which you perform the job. You must understand the purpose of the position you hold and how it fits into the overall goals of the organization. You must be sensitive to what voids would be created if your job were to be eliminated. In the last analysis, you are expected to make a valuable contribution in exchange for a paycheck.

If you are a 'credible' employee, you follow through on tasks until they are satisfactorily completed. Your manager has a need to know that the quality of your performance does not vary from day to day based upon how you feel. She expects that you will "do it right" the first time, or try again until you get it right. She needs to be assured that you truly care about what you are doing and take pride in doing it well.

Taking pride in your work means that you are results-oriented and self-motivated; you are your own most severe critic. Your manager doesn't have a compelling need to look over your shoulder or to constantly supervise your work. She feels secure enough in the relationship, therefore, to grant you the necessary space for completing tasks in an independent fashion. But you must earn this relationship by assuring the manager that you understand the job and possess the determination to complete tasks in the most effective manner possible.

To be successful, you must be a master of the various job procedures that are critical for successful goal accomplishment. On occasion, you may discover a better way to perform a particular task, or identify a procedure that is outdated and in need of revision. Don't hesitate to recommend to your boss the necessary changes so that your job can be accomplished more efficiently. But at the same time, you must be willing to work within the present system until improved procedures are developed and officially accepted into practice.

You should periodically take an objective look at your skills in relation to current demands of the job. Many jobs change and grow as organizations keep pace with an ever advancing technology. To insure that you are not left behind, seize every opportunity to update and consolidate your skills. Your aggressive self-examination of developmental needs and your willingness to stay on top of your field will enhance your chances for survival on the job.

## Exhibit High Character and Personal Credibility

Your job survival depends upon your ability to convince the manager and co-workers that you are an honest, sincere and trustworthy person; you are someone who others can believe in.

The American Management Association recently conducted a study of "Managerial Values and Expectations."[8] They asked 900 managers "What values (personal qualities or behavioral characteristics) do you look for in subordinates, peers, and supervisors?" Two hundred twenty-five different traits were reported by managers; the fifteen most often articulated are listed below in alphabetical order:

**Broadmindedness;** *open-minded, flexible, receptive*

**Competence:** *capable, productive, efficient, thorough*

**Cooperativeness:** *friendly, team player, available, responsive*

**Dependability:** *reliable, conscientious, predictable*

**Determination:** *industrious, hard working, motivated*

**Fairness:** *objective, consistent, democratic*

**Imagination:** *creative, innovative, curious*

**Integrity:** *truthful, trustworthy, has character, has convictions*

**Intelligence:** *bright, thoughtful, logical*

**Leadership:** *inspiring, decisive, provides direction*

**Loyalty:** *has a commitment to me, the company, or policies*

**Maturity:** *experienced, wise, well-grounded, has depth*

**Straight-forwardness:** *direct, candid, forthright*

**Sensitivity:** *appreciative, concerned, aware, respectful*

**Supportive:** *understanding, empathic, helpful*

From this list, managers were asked to choose the *two* characteristics they valued most in employees. Before you read on, see if you can predict the two personal qualities managers deemed most important from this list.

The study indicates that overall, managers consider *integrity* and *competence* to be the most critical factors in determining an employee's value, regardless of the employee's position in the organizational chart. Knowing that integrity is among the most admired qualities in subordinates, peers and managers, you should continuously renew your efforts to establish an image of high character. You should let your boss and co-workers know where you stand on critical organizational issues, speak honestly and directly with people who can assist you in accomplishing your goals, and honor the commitments you make.

## Exercise a Sense of Good Will and Display Allegiance to Your Employer, Department, Manager and Co-Workers

If you want to win support and gain influence within your organization, do everything in your power to grease the results channels for others to succeed. Be supportive of others when they are in need of help and care for their well-being. Be a straight shooter. Share relevant information with your boss and co-workers; actively listen to them. Consider their needs and self-interests as well as your own. Take joy in their successes, and support them in their defeats. Strive for a positive outcome in your relationships. View yourself as a facilitator for individual and group success. Don't expect anything more of your co-workers than you do of yourself; work every bit as hard as they do and execute your job responsibilities in an exemplary fashion.

You can always improve your technical skills by attending various training and development workshops. You can usually improve your job performance by studing various procedures and working on them until you perfect your skills. However, personal qualities such as integrity and goodwill cannot be learned as easily. These qualities transcend the confines of your job. They are contingent upon your character, as developed over a period of time, long before you entered the work force.

Therefore, it is necessary for you to take complete responsibility for vigorously examining how you are perceived by your manager and co-workers. Delve into the reasons why they may think about you as they do and always remember that you are judged not by your intent to do well, but by the effect you have on people in the work place. The impressions others have of you, be they good or bad, right or wrong, exist for a reason. And if you don't like your image, the burden is on you to change it. Therefore, develop a personal "quality control" program on how well you relate to others to insure that you have the necessary support and influence to survive on the job.

## Developing a Power Base

Consider it a number one priority to gain power within your organization. Establishing a power base simply means that you are capable of accomplishing your professional goals through the resources and permission of others. It also means you have developed the necessary skills that will keep you from being jostled about by the games people play at work.

Your power base doesn't come from your position, title, or place on the organizational chart. You don't have to be a boss to carry clout. Nor does power come from how much education or technical training you have. Your power source springs from your personal credibility: you are worthy of belief and when you speak, people listen. Your input is valued. You are able to identify organizational weaknesses, advance solutions and pull people together around a common task. You are a leader.

If you are power-oriented, you place yourself in a pivotal position to make things happen. You don't, however, jump on every bandwagon and respond to every hype. You work on problems that are solvable, where success will reap positive, observable results, where achievement will provide you recognition.

Remember, there exists in every organization a number of critical issues crying out for attention, but no one has seen fit to address them. Whether or not these issues fall within your specific job description is irrelevant. If you have the skills and interest necessary to successfully address these problems, then seize the opportunity to sell your strengths and link them to the needs of the organization.

Pay attention to the changes that are occurring in your organization and ask yourself the question: "What can I do above and beyond my specific job responsibilities to make a greater contribution to my organization." Employees with power don't wait for others to assign them critical functions within the organization. They take the initiative and respond to organizational needs. They simply like getting *involved* and "doing well what needs doing." While they consider their specific job duties to be worthwhile and important, they always keep their eyes open for new opportunities.

If you are interested in building your power base, consider engaging in the following exercise.

1. List those tasks or activities you would like to get into because you have a valuable contribution to make to your department or organization.

2. Indentify specific ways you can contribute to these tasks based upon your talents and interest.

3. Determine what professional developmental steps (additional education and training) will be necessary to justify your involvement in these tasks and activities.

4. Identify the person(s) you have to convince, and develop a plan of action to 'market' your role in these activities.

Before you invest a great deal of time and energy into addressing a particular issue, however, consider the following four criteria for your involvement potential:

**1. Pay Off:** Is my active participation in this activity really worth it? Will it make a significant contribution to the organization? How will my involvement in this activity benefit me? How could it potentially hurt me?

**2. Success Probability:** Is the problem really solvable, or will I be spinning my wheels? Are my suggestions to solve the problem really workable and practical? Will my ideas be accepted considering the people who ultimately decide on the issue?

**3. Degree of Effort:** What will I have to give up or delay to get involved in this activity. How much time and energy will it take to convince others that my ideas will work? If these ideas are accepted, how much effort will be required to implement the plan?

**4. Cost:** Am I equating my ideas to the bottom line of the organization? How much money will it cost? Can the organization afford it? What are the financial risks associated with my plan?

In summary, if you are considering involvement in a problem-solving activity that represents: 1) a big payoff for you and/or the organization, 2) high success probability that your ideas will be acceptable or workable, and 3) low to moderate degree of effort on your part, then "go for it" as long as your plan is cost effective to your organization.

On the other hand, if your potential involvement represents 1) a negligible payoff for you and/or the organization, 2) low success probability that your ideas will be acceptable or workable, and 3) high degree of effort on your part, then regardless of cost, this activity is a set up for frustration and failure.

Don't necessarily attack the biggest organizational problems, but address those issues that are important and that you can affect in some way. Try to visualize the positive difference your efforts will make if you choose to get involved. While you may not be able to solve the whole problem, you may be able to alleviate it in some way. Therefore, try to divide up the problem into smaller parts and commit yourself to getting one or two things done that will make a positive difference.

## Becoming Political

In your attempts to win support and gain influence, identify employees in your organization who already hold power. Then volunteer for activities that place you next to these individuals. Gain their trust and confidence by finding ways to help them succeed in meeting their objectives. Place yourself in a pivotal position to informally negotiate with them: *"I will be glad to do this for you, in exchange I would like. . ."* While these words may never actually be used, your initiatives should be aimed at collecting IOUs from important people for when you need them.

Accept the fact of politics in your organization. Every organization is political, which means that decisions are not always made because it is the "right" or the "good thing to do." There is a world of difference between how things "should be" and how things actually "are" in your organization. And if you believe that your boss or co-workers will always do things because it is the right thing or the good thing to do, you are destined to lead a life of ulcerous, self-righteous disappointment. [9]

Your goal is to survive and thrive on the job. Recognize that some of your activity will be gamesmanship and jockeying for power. There is nothing immoral about this. You can be political and power-oriented without compromising your basic beliefs. You don't have to "sell out" your principles to get ahead. There is nothing cheap or shallow in attending to the self-interests of those persons who can help or hurt the accomplishment of your goals.

If influential people have been willing to do it *for you* in the past, make sure it is in their best interest not to do it *to you* in the future . . . Recognize the fact that people with status expect to be deferred to by employees of lower station. Therefore make it your goal to build effective working relationships with those "heavy weights" as well as all other employees in your organization. Give everyone you deal with, regardless of their position, an opportunity to save face and keep self-esteem intact. It will improve your chances for **On • The • Job • Survival!**

# Notes

# Chapter 9

# CONCLUSION

The productivity crisis has tightened its grip on American industry, and it is not likely to disappear in the near future. As a result, your manager has probably increased her efforts to make certain you give 100% while on the job. She may be demonstrating less patience for employees whose irresponsible communication style destroys group morale or erodes employee confidence in management. She may be increasingly leery of the amount of time spent arbitrating employee feuds or holding meetings for the purpose of motivating employees to work harder.

Your manager may also be questioning the number of employees it really takes to get the job done. As she is expected to increase productivity with fewer resources at her command, she may have discovered that a lean department has some advantages: fewer employees don't get into each other's way; they have room to move without colliding into one another. They can do their work without having to explain it all the time. They are too busy to complain.

Because of the demands on her time, perhaps your manager has become a task master and stickler for detail as she audits the quality of your work. She simply cannot afford to compromise her high standards or be expected to understand when you have a bad day or are in a foul mood. Indeed, she is so busy attending to her own managerial responsibilities that she may, on occasion, inadvertantly neglect to meet your psychological needs.

Today's harsh economic realities may have forced your manager to recognize that warm feelings and pleasant words are meaningless unless they result in improved performance; that good employee relations is not a goal in itself, but a *means* to achieve a better product. You may believe that your job should always be meaningful, or that your employer should provide a working environment that is professionally rewarding. But attaining the "good life" on the job is not an inalienable right. To survive and thrive on the job, *you* must take the major responsibility for attaining effectiveness and fulfillment at work. Job success and satisfaction are ultimately in your hands.

# Illustrations

## Indicators of Credible Employees

- They demonstrate total commitment to the job.
- They are results/achievement-oriented.
- They get things done by gaining cooperation of boss and co-workers.
- They manage their time well.
- They make offers of assistance to others in need without being asked for help.
- They are generally satisfied with the work they do and show it.
- They volunteer to participate in activities that make a valuable contribution to the organization even if the task is not mentioned in their job description.
- They effectively "package" their ideas to win support and influence people.
- They maintain self-esteem and professionalism regardless how others behave.
- They don't fail often, but when they do, they fail gracefully.
- They can say "no" without making co-workers defensive.
- They maintain confidentiality and stay out of other people's business.
- They are persons others turn to for support or guidance.
- They have established realistic expectations of themselves and others.
- They like happy endings and good completions.
- They try to set things right, to clean up bad situations without being dogmatic or arrogant in the process.
- They notice positive qualities in boss and co-workers and compliment others whenever appropriate.
- They generally pick their own causes (which are apt to be few in number) rather than respond to every hype.
- They somehow manage to like their work as it is, yet simultaneously try to improve it.
- They strive for efficiency. They work toward making their work area neater, simpler, faster, safer, more productive.
- They strive for constructive working relationships regardless of their personal feelings toward co-workers or boss.
- They take responsibility for their own success and satisfaction on the job.
- They demonstrate the capacity for patience, staying power and tolerance.

| Your Chances for Job Survival Are Good if: | You Stand a Chance of Losing Your Job if: |
|---|---|
| 1. You take responsibility for your own success or failure. You are self-critical regarding the quality of your work. You are always in search of new ways to improve your job performance. | You search for alibis when a mistake is made. You don't take responsibility for the problems you face. You get defensive when given feedback on how to improve your work. |
| 2. You try to establish a win-win relationship with your manager and co-workers. You strive to help them succeed and look good on the job. | You are only concerned about yourself. |
| 3. You understand your manager's leadership "style", and you try to work effectively within it. You maximize your manager's strengths and minimize her weaknesses. You use your manager as a resource for accomplishing your goals. | You are insensitive to your manager's needs and expectations. You respond only to what's convenient or comfortable for you. You call attention to your manager's limitations and dismiss her strengths. You delight in her failures, and you find subtle ways to embarrass or inconvience her. |
| 4. You give your manager the benefit of the doubt when an unpopular decision is made. You check out her reasons and consider them seriously. | You question your manager's intentions and impugn her integrity. You polarize employees from the manager by bad-mouthing her at every opportunity. |
| 5. You initiate conversations with your manager to determine how well you are doing on the job. | You choose to remain in doubt regarding the quality of your performance. You allow yourself to wallow in ambiguity or paranoia, not knowing where you stand with your boss. |

| Your Chances for Job Survival Are Good if: | You Stand a Chance of Losing Your Job if: |
|---|---|
| 6. You take initiative whenever possible. You demonstrate a willingness to "go the extra mile" to get the job done. You "do well what needs doing" without being asked and without constant supervision. | You're reactive and do only what you consider to be within your job scope. You do just enough to get by. |
| 7. When you have a problem, you ask for what you want or need. You talk directly to those persons who can help. | When you have a problem, you talk to everyone *but* those individuals who can help. You gossip and backstab. |
| 8. You are able to adjust to those problems on the job that no one can do anything about. You're selective regarding which issues you address. | You "go to the mat" on everything. You view all problems as critical and demand immediate resolutions. |
| 9. When in conflict, you maintain self control. You confront others in a private, confidential setting. You discuss differences of opinion in a way that maximizes the chance for reaching an acceptable resolution. | When in conflict, you lead with your emotions and throw caution to the wind. You blurt out whatever comes to mind. You shoot from the hip. You dig in your heels and prepare to fight. You play public win/lose games and provide no face-saving for those with whom you disagree. |
| 10. You follow-through on the commitments you make. You're a person of your word. You work effectively with your manager and co-workers regardless of whether you personally like them. | You bluff and threaten to get your way. You display the attitude; "I don't like her, so I can't (won't) work with her." |

| How To Minimize Defensiveness/Hostility In Co-Workers | How To Create Defensiveness/Hostility In Co-Workers |
|---|---|
| 1. Change one's own behavior first, making it easier for the co-worker to change in the direction you want. | Insist that the co-worker change his belief or behavior without any change on your part. |
| 2. Speak to the co-worker as an adult and as a professional with an equal stake in the improvement of the working relationship. | Come across as superior in thinking or attitude. Talk down to the co-worker. |
| 3. Be flexible in your position. Allow for adjustment in your thinking and behavior, based upon the co-worker's feedback. | Demonstrate that "my way of seeing the problem is the only way." |

| How To Minimize Defensiveness/Hostility In Co-Workers | How To Create Defensiveness/Hostility In Co-Workers |
|---|---|
| 4. Be sensitive to road blocks the co-worker may face. Initiate offers of assistance to help him overcome them. | Show lack of concern for co-worker's constraints or limitations. |
| 5. Feedback to the co-worker is direct, honest, constructive and informative. It should be two-way with both parties benefiting from the discussion. | Try to change the co-worker through deception, manipulation or undermining. |
| 6. Instead of attacking the co-worker, describe non-judgmentally what you see or hear him doing. Carefully explain how his actions affect you. | Judge co-worker's competence or wisdom. |

# Packaging Your Ideas for Change

Don't assume that your 'great' idea for a change will go un-contested because it's the right thing or the good thing to do. Anticipate and plan for resistance to your idea so that you can be more persuasive. Below are typical manager and co-worker responses in defense of "keeping things the way they are." Before you present your idea, make certain that you can address these concerns.

## Concerns for Having to do Something New or Different

**A.** What's the *need* for a change?

**B.** We've always done it this way.

**C.** What we're doing now is working and we're satisfied.

**D.** What's the evidence that anything will be better?

**E.** Have you assessed the possible side effects or the negative consequences of the change?

## Concerns for Practicality

**A.** Will it take more time?

**B.** This represents more paperwork; will it really help us?

**C.** I'm already overloaded doing too many other things.

**D.** What will I have to give up?

## Concerns for Being Included

**A.** Will you listen to alternatives?

**B.** Am I going to have input on the "how to?"

## Direct, Overt Rejections

**A.** It won't work.

**B.** I can't see the payoff.

**C.** This will be a waste of time.

## Fears of Change for the Sake of Change Itself

**A.** I've tried that before.

**B** Feels like "here we go again."

**C.** By the time we change everything, time will be ripe for another change.

## Fear of Failure

**A.** What new things will I have to learn and will I be able to learn them?

**B.** What kind of help will I get to make the change?

**C.** Will I be responsible if it fails?

## "Yes . . . But" Responses

**A.** I like your ideas, but the others won't buy them.

**B.** We're different/special; that won't work for us.

**C.** The regulations/rules won't let us do that ("they" won't let us).

**D.** We don't have the money.

**E.** Where has it worked?

"Utilizing Resistance as a Constructive Resource for Change"
Address by Ronald Lippitt at the American Society of Training & Development.
National Conference, May 20, 1983, San Antonio, Texas.

# Most Common Irritating Employee Behaviors As Described By Managers

**Apathetic & De-motivated:** "The employee is practicing 'OJR' (On-the-Job-Retirement). He seems to be "putting in his time" while maintaining a minimally acceptable productivity level. He is passive and unenthusiastic about his work. He doesn't ask questions when unclear about something. He either assumes he knows what to do and makes mistakes, or he sits around waiting for someone to explain it to him. The employee also passes the buck on problems and exhibits the 'It's not my job' syndrome. He is an avid clock-watcher. He demonstrates an inability or an unwillingness to change with the times. He just doesn't seem to care."

**Listless:** "The employee has difficulty focusing attention on his work. He doesn't follow instructions or complete tasks such as submitting unfinished reports and returning phone calls. He either procrastinates on activities that should be done immediately, or takes short-cuts on operating procedures to save time."

**Unsure:** "The employee has lost confidence in himself which is causing him to make more mistakes. He is having trouble keeping up with the work pace. He is creating a dependency relationship on co-workers and they are beginning to resent having to pick up the slack."

**Self Centered:** "When completed with his own work, the employee doesn't make offers of assistance to others in need of help."

**Withdrawn:** "The employee avoids me and acts as if he wants as little to do with me as possible. He rarely says "hello" or "good-bye," much less engage in small talk when the situation permits. He does not consult with me on matters of importance. Indeed, he withholds from me critical information needed to make decisions."

**Confrontive:** "The employee becomes quite irritated when I ask him a question or provide direction. He makes it plain that he doesn't like me. He goes over my head with problems when I could be of help. When he does approach me with a problem, he is combative, and he frequently challenges my authority in full view of others."

**Subversive:** "The employee seems to be competing for my leadership. I'm suspicious that he's talking behind my back and causing dissension. He makes mountains out of molehills and is raising havoc with group morale."

**Unpredictable:** "One day he's fine and everything is sweetness and light. When things are going well for him, he often engages in excessive talking with fellow workers, preventing even the most well-motivated employees from completing their work. But on other days when his mood is foul, watch out! *Anyone* who gets in his way is in trouble."

**Not at work as schedule requires:** "The employee's quality of work is first rate, but his excessive absenteeism is unacceptable. He has established a pattern of frequent one or two day absences and is often gone before or after a scheduled day off. Whether he is really sick or not is irrelevant. I need him here on a regular basis so that the work can get done. His irregular attendance sets a poor example and places a burden on others who must work harder to compensate for his absences." *(Note: Absenteeism and tardiness are the most often articulated reasons that managers give for terminating an employee.)*

# Footnotes

1. Ellis, Albert E. and Harper, Robert A., *A New Guide to Rational Living,* Hollywood, California: Wilshire Book Company. 1975 (p. 130)

2. ibid

3. ibid

4. Hegarty, Richard, *How To Manage Your Boss,* Mill Valley, California: Whatever Publishing Company, 1982

5. ibid

6. Piaget, Gerard W. and Binkley, Barbara, *How To Communicate Under Pressure: Dealing Effectively with Difficult People.* Portola Valley, California: IAHB Press, 1982

7. Haney, William, *Communication & Organizational Behavior,* Homewood, Illinois: Richard D. Irwin, Inc., (p. 179)

8. Schmidt, W. & Posner, B., *Managerial Values & Expectations,* Chicago, Illinois: American Management Association, 1982

9. Wydra, Frank T. "Power & the HRD Pro," *Training: The Magazine of Human Resource Development,* August, 1981, (p. 26-31)

This book may also be ordered by mail from the publisher.

Please send me **ON THE JOB SURVIVAL.** I am enclosing 9.95 (6.95 plus $3.00 per copy to cover postage and handling). Send check or money order — no cash or C.O.D.'s to:

**Canoe Press**
**P.O. Box 174**
**Oak Park, Illinois 60303**

Name _____

Organization _____

Address _____

City _____ State _____ Zip _____

*Inquire about special rate for quantity orders.*